Inside the Water Cycle

William B. Rice

Earth and Space Science Readers:
Inside the Water Cycle

Publishing Credits

Editorial Director
Dona Herweck Rice

Associate Editor
Joshua BishopRoby

Editor-in-Chief
Sharon Coan, M.S.Ed.

Creative Director
Lee Aucoin

Illustration Manager
Timothy J. Bradley

Publisher
Rachelle Cracchiolo, M.S.Ed.

Science Contributor
Sally Ride Science

Science Consultants
Nancy McKeown,
Planetary Geologist
William B. Rice,
Engineering Geologist

Teacher Created Materials
5301 Oceanus Drive
Huntington Beach, CA 92649-1030
http://www.tcmpub.com
ISBN 978-0-7439-0555-8

Table of Contents

Down Came the Rain

Rain has been falling hard for hours, but now it's starting to slow. Bit by bit, the drum of rain on the windowpane lessens. It becomes a soft drizzle until finally, a single drop strikes. Slowly it glides down the glass. At the edge, it stops for a minute and then, plop! It drops to a puddle on the ground.

The sky is still covered in clouds, but the puddle slowly disappears. The water sinks into the soil, leaving mud behind. When the sun comes out, the mud disappears. There is no sign of the water, and no sign of the rain that poured for hours. It seems like the water just never existed. But it did, and it still does. It exists in other forms and other places. It is somewhere within the **water cycle.**

Rain that falls from the sky will seem to disappear over time, but it still exists somewhere in some form.

Plants use rainwater to grow.

'Round and 'Round We Go

The seasons, the days of the week, and the circle of life all have one thing in common. They are **cycles**. They move from one phase to another and then back to the beginning. It's something like playing a game of Monopoly that never ends. Cycles follow the path from one place to another and back around again.

The truth is that cycles don't really have a start or finish. They keep going like a circle. A circle has no start or end. The same is true for the water cycle. Water moves from one phase to the next.

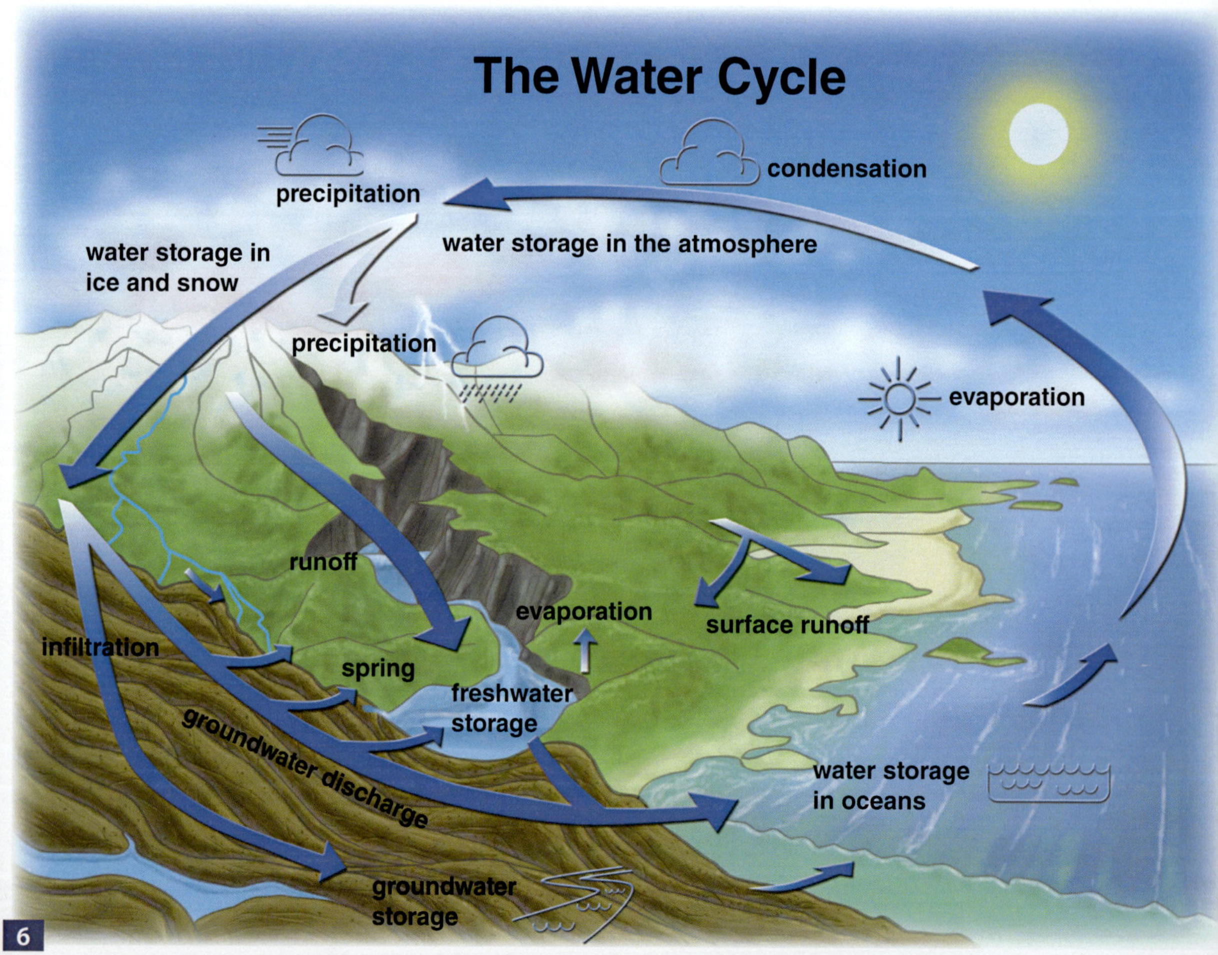

But water is just water—isn't it? How can it have phases? That's easy. Water is a **compound**. That means it is made of more than one **element**. An element is a naturally occurring substance. The elements that make water are hydrogen and oxygen.

Two hydrogen **atoms** combine with one oxygen atom to make one tiny **molecule** of water. This is written as H_2O. Billions of water molecules combine to make the liquid substance you know of as water.

H_2O doesn't have to be just a liquid. It can also be as solid as ice. It can be a gas as steam or vapor. No matter what, it's still water. It just changes form as it moves through the water cycle.

Water comes in many forms: steam, ice, snow, tiny water drops, and giant waterfalls!

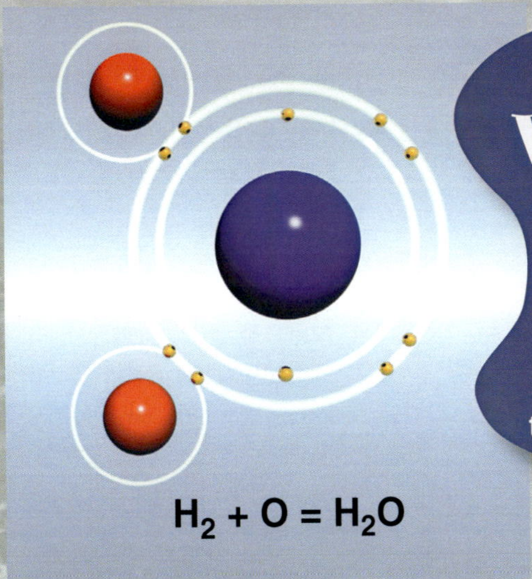

Water Molecule

You can't see a water molecule unless you have a very powerful microscope. This diagram gives the idea of what a water molecule is like. You can see the hydrogen and oxygen atoms bonded together to form a molecule.

Evaporation into the Sky

There's really no start to the water cycle. To understand it, we must begin somewhere. We'll start with **evaporation**.

Water covers seventy percent of Earth's surface. Most of this water is in oceans. Evaporation is how water in the ocean and elsewhere on Earth's surface gets into clouds in the air.

Evaporation happens everywhere. When a liquid is heated enough, it changes to a gas. This happens when the heated molecules move around so fast they are no longer close enough together to be a part of the liquid. When water evaporates, we call it steam or water vapor. It happens on a small scale when a stove heats a pot of water. It happens on a very large scale when the sun heats water in the oceans.

When the oceans are heated by the sun, some water becomes vapor. The vapor goes up into Earth's atmosphere. This happens all across the world every day. It is a very big process. In fact, this heating of ocean water is the driving force of Earth's weather.

Rainbows form when sunlight hits molecules of water in the air. The water breaks the light into the color spectrum.

Water is used to grow almost every food you eat.

What's the Big Deal?

Water is a very big deal. Think about how you used water just today. You brushed your teeth, bathed, and used the restroom. You drank some water, too. These are just a few of the simple ways that people use water. We also use water to grow crops to eat and to give to our pets and livestock to drink. We use it in business and industry for both washing and making things. It's used by wildlife for drinking, and plants in the wilderness need it to grow. Fish and other animals live in it. These are just some of the things for which water is used. The important thing about water is that no living thing can survive without it.

Condensation and Cloud Formation

As the water vapor moves up through the **atmosphere**, it begins to lose the heat it had taken in. When it loses enough heat, the vapor turns back into a liquid. This process is called **condensation**. The water molecules start sticking together, and they form small droplets or ice crystals. The droplets or crystals are very tiny and not heavy enough to fall back to Earth. When there are enough of them close together, they can form clouds. Clouds are simply dense groups of water droplets or ice crystals. The light of the sun hits them and reflects off of them. We see this as a cloud.

The wind in the atmosphere blows the clouds over the land. We see clouds like this nearly every day. Sometimes, while driving high in the mountains, you might even drive right through a cloud.

They may look solid, but clouds are made of water vapor.

Cloud Types

The names of clouds are based on their shapes, sizes, and height or altitude. There are many types of clouds. Some common types are named, described, and pictured in this chart.

Cloud	Description	
cirrus	thin, long, white, wispy clouds at high altitudes and made of ice crystals	
altostratus	middle-lying, gray clouds spread widely like a big sheet	
stratus	flat, gray, layered clouds	
cumulonimbus	tall, dense, gray, puffy storm clouds	
cumulus	tall, puffy, white clouds	

Cloud Movement

When you watch a cloud in the sky long enough, you'll see it move and change shape. Sometimes clouds almost seem to race by. Once a cloud forms, what causes it to move from the place it forms to someplace else? Why doesn't it stay put?

Wind and air pressure squeeze these clouds into long shapes.

These clouds are spread out by the same forces.

When the sun hits Earth, it doesn't heat evenly. Some places get hotter than other places do. This causes pressure differences in the air. To make up for these differences, air moves from areas with high pressure to areas with low pressure. This is how wind happens. Also, the spinning of Earth and currents in the oceans can affect movement of the air on Earth as well. This process of air moving from side to side across the earth is called **advection**.

Child's Play

Almost everyone has looked at a cloud and imagined something pictured there. As the cloud changes shape, so does the image. Just for fun, take a look at these clouds. What do you see in them?

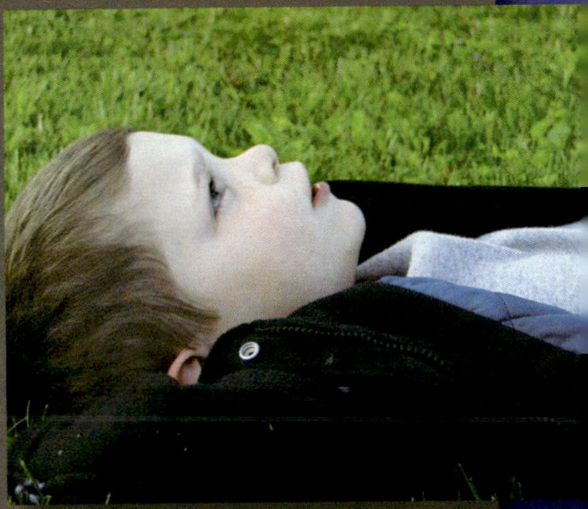

Precipitation

Water vapor in the atmosphere can form water droplets or turn into solid ice crystals. The wind and air movement can cause these particles to bump into each other. When that happens, they form larger particles. If they get large enough, they will fall to the earth. When they fall, it is called **precipitation**. Of course, precipitation is better known as rain, **snow**, **sleet**, and **hail**. Each of these usually falls to the earth in some type of storm. Sometimes the storms are small and gentle. Many times they are big, fierce, and dangerous. Fiercer storms are such things as **hurricanes** and blizzards.

Precipitation happens over both the oceans and the land. Sometimes precipitation doesn't always hit the surface of the earth. In some places where the air is hot and dry near the ground, the raindrops evaporate before touching land. This is an unusual occurrence called **virga**. It happens mainly in desert regions.

Raindrops called virga never get to the ground.

Hurricanes

A **hurricane** is a severe tropical storm. It is the biggest kind of storm that forms on Earth. In some parts of the world, a hurricane is called a typhoon or cyclone. To be called a hurricane, the winds within the storm have to reach 119 kilometers (74 miles) or more per hour. Hurricanes carry a great deal of water. When they move onto land, they are massively destructive. For example, Hurricane Katrina in 2005 destroyed thousands of homes, buildings, and businesses. Countless lives were lost or upset. However, hurricanes are an important part of the water cycle. A big key to the water cycle is the movement of water. Hurricanes move a lot of water at once. This also releases a great deal of built up energy in Earth's oceans and atmosphere.

a snow-covered scene

Snow

Throw it, build with it, slide on it, or catch it on your tongue—snow can be a lot of fun! The truth is that snow is just another form of water. It is precipitation of ice crystals, and the ice crystals are water in a solid form. Snow forms when the air is very cold and there is a great deal of water vapor in it.

The ice crystals in snow can be piled on top of each other to build snowmen.

Sleet

Not many people take pleasure in sleet. Sleet is another form of frozen water. It is actually tiny frozen raindrops or ice pellets. It is often mistaken for hail. It forms in a different way, though. Sometimes falling raindrops may pass through a layer of warm air in the atmosphere and then freeze when passing through a layer of cold air. In this way, they form tiny ice balls that hit the ground. This is called sleet.

sleet on the hood of a car

ice crystals

Hail

Hail forms in thunderstorm clouds when supercooled water freezes on contact with dust particles, bugs, or ice crystals. These particles are called *nuclei*. Layers of ice can grow very quickly around the nuclei when there are large numbers of these supercooled water droplets. These ice balls are called hailstones. When they become too heavy for the winds inside a cloud to hold them up, they plummet to the ground. This is called a hailstorm. Hailstones can range in size from something like a pea to the size of a softball. As you can imagine, when large hailstones fall, they can cause a lot of destruction and even deaths.

Water on the Earth

Water enters the next phase of the water cycle once it hits the ground. Many things can happen, depending on where it falls and in what form. If the water is frozen as snow, sleet, or hail, it might pile up and stay frozen for awhile. It may melt quickly and change to liquid water. When water falls as rain, it can soak into the ground or it can run off and form streams or rivers. Eventually, all the water will make its way back to the ocean. It may be a short trip of just a few days, or it may be a long trip of hundreds or even thousands of years.

The ocean stores 97% of Earth's water. Less than 1% of Earth's water is liquid freshwater.

Fresh or Salt?

Water that falls from the sky is called freshwater. Water in the ocean is called saltwater.

The Wonder of Waterfalls

Waterfalls happen when water flows over a sharp drop in the earth's surface. They can be quite small or very large. They are found all over the world. People come from all over to see them. Many people think they are among the most beautiful and amazing landforms on Earth. Here are some well-known waterfalls from around the world.

Waterfall	Place	Description	
Victoria Falls	border of Zimbabwe and Zambia	largest single sheet of water in the world, 1.7 kilometers (1.06 miles) wide	
Angel Falls	Venezuela	highest free-leaping fall, 979 meters (3,212 feet)	
Iguazu Falls	border of Brazil and Argentina	consists of almost 300 falls	
Niagara Falls	border of Canada and the United States	most powerful fall in North America; perhaps most famous waterfall in the world	

Snow on the Ground, Glaciers, and Icecaps

This river is fed by snowmelt.

Snow that falls on the ground will usually stay frozen and pile up. After a few months, when the air warms during spring, the snow begins to melt. It turns back to a liquid state. This water is called **snowmelt**. Snowmelt will either run off into a river, lake, or stream, or it will soak into the ground.

glacier

In some areas, it is so cold year-round that snow does not melt. In fact, it piles up year after year and can become very thick and deep. Because of the weight of the snow, it **compacts** and becomes ice. This happens in such places as Antarctica and Greenland and on very high mountains. In fact, the snow in Antarctica and Greenland has piled up hundreds of meters (thousands of feet) thick. It also covers several hundred square kilometers (miles). When snow piles in this way, it is called an **icecap**. The oldest snow in Antarctica is 740,000 years old. The oldest snow in Greenland is 250,000 years old.

In some mountains, this snow and ice is not spread over a wide area but piles up in valleys. When the ice and snow gets heavy enough, it begins slowly to move downhill. When this happens, the formation is called a **glacier**. A glacier can be several kilometers (or miles) long and look something like a river of ice.

When the lowest end of a glacier gets warm enough, it melts into liquid water. The water flows like a river or stream. When the edges of an icecap or glacier meet the ocean, large chunks of ice may break into the water. These are called **icebergs**.

At some point in the water cycle, water may flow in rivers and streams.

Throughout time, people have found groundwater by digging wells.

Rain, Rivers, and Groundwater

Water that falls from the sky in liquid form is called rain. Whenever it rains, water soaks into the ground. It flows through the small spaces between the soil particles in the ground. Deeper underground, the rock is solid and the water can't flow through it. So, all the small spaces in the soil begin to fill up. When there is enough water, it flows horizontally. Water that soaks into the ground like this is called **groundwater**.

People have known about groundwater for thousands of years. They have learned how to get this water from the ground and bring it to the surface. The water is used for drinking and for watering plants and crops.

If there is a lot of water during a rainstorm, all the water can't soak into the ground. Instead, the rainwater runs over the ground's surface and into streams and rivers. These streams and rivers flow into larger streams and rivers or lakes. As the water flows, people sometimes use it for drinking and giving water to plants and animals. Eventually, all the water makes its way back to the ocean.

Henry Darcy

Bringing Water to the People

Today, we expect that when we turn a faucet, water will flow freely. For people in the past, it wasn't always that way. People would catch rain in barrels as it ran off their roofs. They would dig wells and pull their water up from the ground. Water would be carried in wagons from places farther away. In the 1830s, a French scientist named Henry Darcy designed a system that brought water right to people in their homes. He did it in his hometown of Dijon, France. It was one of the first cities to have such a system. Darcy did other important experiments with water flow, too. The people of Dijon were so thankful for what he did that they honored him with a monument in the center of town.

Because the reservoir was at a higher altitude than the city, Darcy could build fountains that used gravity to shoot water into the air. The people of Dijon drew water from fountains like this.

Water in Oceans

Once water flows to the oceans, it has come the full circle of the water cycle. All the water that flows into the ocean once evaporated out of the ocean. Molecule after molecule of water leaves its ocean bed and, one day, returns to its old home.

It's hard to say what might happen to any one molecule of water once it arrives in the ocean. It might evaporate right away or years later. It might flow down into the ocean depths. It might be carried by currents to different parts of the world.

It might arrive at a polar area and freeze. It might soak into the bathing suit of someone like you, swimming along the shore!

Whatever the case, one thing is guaranteed. The molecule will continue on its path through the water cycle.

All rivers flow downhill to the ocean.

Where the Amazon Meets the Atlantic

The Amazon River is not the longest river in the world, but it carries more water than any other river does. In fact, it empties so much water into the ocean that where the Amazon meets the Atlantic Ocean, there is still freshwater about 200 kilometers (125 miles) offshore.

the Amazon River as seen from space

Wonderful Water

Because of the water cycle, life can be found just about everywhere on Earth. Every living thing needs water to survive. Some things may not drink water, but they still need water to live. Water is the most vital, crucial substance on Earth. In fact, Earth is what it is because of water in all its changing forms.

The water cycle makes life interesting. We get to play and slide in the snow. We splash in rain puddles. We enjoy beautiful clouds that make spectacular sunsets and sunrises. We go rafting on rivers and lakes. We enjoy the waves at the beach. Why? Wonderful water in all its forms makes it all possible!

waterskier

Water can be lots of fun!

Water in Space

Astronauts in space need water, too. But it is expensive to keep sending water from Earth to astronauts working and living in space. On the International Space Station, scientists have installed a machine that processes water. It recycles water by collecting, cleaning, and purifying it. Astronauts use water to drink, brush their teeth, and wash themselves. The astronauts also release water when they exhale and when they go to the bathroom. The water machine collects all of this water and recycles it to be used again. In a way, it is a small water cycle.

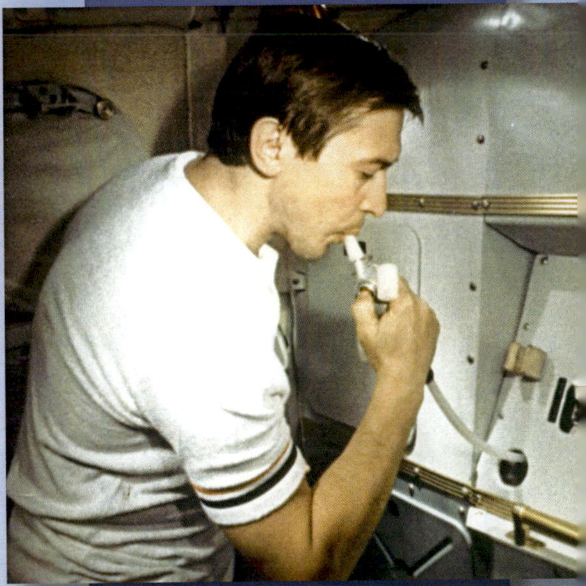

Lab: *How Water Soaks into the Earth*

When it rains, water soaks into the earth. The size of the particles in the soil affects how fast the water soaks in. Why does this matter? More water can soak in faster with certain kinds of soil. This helps the water supply for the people in the area. It can also make certain areas less likely to flood.

Materials

- water
- measuring cup
- coffee can or similar container
- sand
- unpopped popcorn
- pebbles or gravel (about the size of marbles)
- thin tool to make a hole in the can
- stopwatch or a watch with a second hand
- paper and pencil

Procedure

1 Make a hole in the side of the can near the bottom. The hole should be about 2 to 3 millimeters ($\frac{1}{8}$ to $\frac{1}{4}$ inch) big. Be careful! Have an adult help with this.

2 Cover the hole with your finger. Fill the can with sand up to 2.5 cm (1 inch) from the top.

3 Fill the measuring cup with water. Slowly pour it over the sand so that it soaks in. Keep adding water until it doesn't soak into the sand anymore. Important: Keep track of the amount of water you pour into the sand.

4 Get your watch ready. Remove your finger from the hole and start timing. (You may want to place the can in the sink or on the sink's edge so the water flows into it.) Stop timing when there is about one drip of water per second coming out of the can. Record the result in a chart.

5 Empty the contents of the can. Wash the can well with water so there is no sand left.

6 Repeat steps 2–5 with the popcorn and then with the pebbles or gravel. For each, use the same amount of water as with the sand. Don't worry about the water soaking in.

7 Compare the results. Through which substance does the water flow fastest? Slowest?

Extension

To extend this activity, measure water flow through each substance three times in a row. Compare those results. Is there a big difference between the water's flow the first time through the substance and the second and third times? Also, you can catch the water that runs out and measure it to compare its volume. Why doesn't all of the water flow out from each substance?

Glossary

advection—the horizontal movement of an air mass

altostratus—bluish or gray clouds in sheets or layers

atmosphere—the mixture of gases that surrounds a planet; the air

atom—the smallest component of an element having the chemical properties of the element

cirrus—a light, feathery cloud high in the sky

compact—pressed tightly together

compound—a pure chemical substance composed of simpler substances

condensation—gas turning into liquid

cumulonimbus—an extremely dense, vertical cumulus cloud

cumulus—a tall, white cloud with a wide, flat base and rounded shape

cycle—a repeated sequence of events

element—a simple substance that cannot be reduced to simpler substances by chemical means

evaporation—liquid turning into gas

freshwater—water that is not salty

glacier—a large mass of ice on land

groundwater—water beneath the earth's surface

hail—a frozen form of precipitation

hurricane—a tropical cyclone with heavy rains and winds exceeding 120 km/hr

iceberg—a very large mass of ice that floats in the sea

icecap—a large dome of ice that gathers on the poles of a planet

molecule—the simplest unit of a chemical substance, usually a group of two or more atoms

precipitation—water that falls from the clouds

saltwater—water with salt in it, as in the ocean

sleet—frozen raindrops

snow—frozen crystals of water that fall from the sky

snowmelt—the runoff of melting snow

stratus—a horizontal layer of gray clouds

virga—rain that evaporates before it reaches the ground

water cycle—the cycle of evaporation and condensation that moves water around the Earth

waterfall—water, especially from a river or stream, dropping from a higher to a lower point

Index

Sally Ride Science

Sally Ride Science™ is an innovative content company dedicated to fueling young people's interests in science. Our publications and programs provide opportunities for students and teachers to explore the captivating world of science—from astrobiology to zoology. We bring science to life and show young people that science is creative, collaborative, fascinating, and fun.

Image Credits

Cover: Photos.com; p.3 Judy Tan; p.4 (top) Ljupco Smokovski/Shutterstock; p.4–5 Photos.com; p.5 (top) Andrew Chin/Shutterstock; p.5 (bottom) Stuart Cuss/Shutterstock; p.6 (top) Mike Rogal/Shutterstock; p.6 (bottom) Tim Bradley; p.7 (background) Judy Tan; p.7 (clockwise from left) Michael Pemberton/Shutterstock; Chepe Nicoli/Shutterstock; Mike Rogal/Shutterstock; Joy Fera/Shutterstock; p.7 (bottom) Tim Bradley; p.8 (top) iStockphoto; p.8 (right) Tim Bradley; p.8 (bottom) Photos.com; p.9 Sally Scott/Shutterstock; p.10 (top) Christophe Testi/Shutterstock; p.10 (right) Tim Bradley; p.10 (bottom) Christophe Testi/Shutterstock; p.11 (background) Bruce Amos/Shutterstock; p.11 (top to bottom) NOAA (4); p.12 (top) NOAA; p.12 (right) Tim Bradley; p.12 (bottom) NOAA; p.12–13 (background) Photos.com; p.12–13 John E Marriott/Alamy; p.13 (top) Florea Marius Catalin/Shutterstock; p.13 (right) Linda Armstrong/Shutterstock; p.13 (bottom) Heidi Dp/Dreamstime.com; p.14 (top) Ustyuzhanin Andrey Anatolyevitch/Shutterstock; p.14 (right) Tim Bradley; p.14 (bottom) Gordon Garradd/Photo Researchers, Inc.; p.15 Dr. Robert Muntefering/Getty Images; p.16 (top) SuperStock, Inc./SuperStock; p.16 (left) Rene Jansa/Shutterstock; p.16 (right) OlgaLis/Shutterstock; p.17 (top) Adrian Hughes/Dreamstime.com; p.17 (bottom) Ed Endicott/Dreamstime.com; p.18 (top) Ishbukar Yalilfatar/Shutterstock; p.18 (right) Tim Bradley; p.18 (bottom) Photos.com; p.19 (background) Mike Norton/Shutterstock; p.19 (top to bottom) Photos.com; Photos.com; Shutterstock; iStockphoto; p.20 (top) Vladi/Shutterstock; p.20 (bottom) Photos.com; p.21 Nik Niklz/Shutterstock; p.22 (top) Tina Rencelj/Shutterstock; p.22 (bottom) Jesper Jensen/Alamy; p.23 (top) Courtesy of Henry Darcy Family; p.23 (bottom) Tim Bradley; p.24 (top) Photos.com; p.24 (right) Tim Bradley; p.24–25 Photos.com; p.25 (bottom) M-Sat Ltd/Photo Researchers, Inc.; p.26 (top) Rene Jansa/Shutterstock; p.26 (left) Anita Patterson Peppers/Shutterstock; p.26 (bottom) Photos.com; p.26–27 Photos.com; p.27 (right) NASA; p.28 (top) Tony Wear/Shutterstock; p.28–29 Nicoll Rager Fuller